# A Note to Parents

DK READERS is a compelling program for beginning readers, designed in conjunction with leading literacy experts, including Dr. Linda Gambrell, Distinguished Professor of Education at Clemson University. Dr. Gambrell has served as President of the National Reading Conference, the College Reading Association, and the International Reading Association.

Beautiful illustrations and superb full-color photographs combine with engaging, easy-to-read stories to offer a fresh approach to each subject in the series. Each DK READER is guaranteed to capture a child's interest while developing his or her reading skills, general knowledge, and love of reading.

The five levels of DK READERS are aimed at different reading abilities, enabling you to choose the books that are exactly right for your child:

**Pre-level 1:** Learning to read
**Level 1:** Beginning to read
**Level 2:** Beginning to read alone
**Level 3:** Reading alone
**Level 4:** Proficient readers

The "normal" age at which a child begins to read can be anywhere from three to eight years old. Adult participation through the lower levels is very helpful for providing encouragement, discussing storylines, and sounding out unfamiliar words.

No matter which level you select, you can be sure that you are helping your child learn to read, then read to learn!

LONDON, NEW YORK, MUNICH,
MELBOURNE, AND DELHI

**Editor** Pamela Afram
**Project Art Editor** Clive Savage
**Managing Editor** Laura Gilbert
**Design Manager** Maxine Pedliham
**Art Director** Ron Stobbart
**Publisher** Simon Beecroft
**Publishing Director** Alex Allan
**Pre-Production Producer** Rebecca Fallowfield
**Senior Producer** Shabana Shakir
**Jacket Designer** Satvir Sihota

Designed and edited by Tall Tree Ltd
**Designer** Malcolm Parchment
**Editor** Jon Richards

**Reading Consultant** Linda B. Gambrell, Ph.D.

**For Lucasfilm**
**Executive Editor** Jonathan W. Rinzler
**Art Director** Troy Alders
**Keeper of the Holocron** Leland Chee
**Director of Publishing** Carol Roeder

First American Edition, 2013
10 9 8 7 6 5 4 3 2 1
Published in the United States by DK Publishing
375 Hudson Street, New York, New York 10014

DK books are available at special discounts when purchased in bulk
for sales promotions, premiums, fund-raising, or educational use.
For details, contact:
DK Publishing Special Markets
375 Hudson Street, New York, New York 10014
SpecialSales@dk.com

A catalog record for this book is available
from the Library of Congress.

ISBN: 978-1-4654-0585-2 (Paperback)
ISBN: 978-1-4654-0586-9 (Hardcover)

Color reproduction by Alta Image
Printed and bound in China by L.Rex

Discover more at
**www.dk.com**
**www.starwars.com**

# Contents

# DK READERS

# STAR WARS

## THE CLONE WARS

# Masters of the Force

Written by Jon Richards

These warriors are
Masters of the Force.
They use a special
power called the Force.

The Force makes them
very strong fighters.
It also gives them
special talents.

# Masters of the Force can be good or bad.

Obi-Wan Kenobi

Mace Windu

# The good ones are called the Jedi.

**Ahsoka Tano**

**Anakin Skywalker**

Yoda

This is Jedi
Grand Master Yoda.
He is using the Force
to fight battle droids.

Yoda (YOH-DAH)

lightsaber

# This is Jedi Knight Anakin Skywalker.

**Anakin Skywalker**

**starfighter**

Anakin Skywalker
(AN-A-KIN SKY-WAH-KER)

He is using the Force
to fly a starfighter
with amazing skill.

11

This is Jedi Master
Mace Windu.

clone trooper

Mace Windu
(MAYSS WIN-DOO)

He is using the Force
to shatter a windshield
to save a clone trooper.

**gunship**

Quinlan Vos
(QWIN-LAN VOS)

This is Jedi Master
Quinlan Vos.
He is using the Force
to jump from a gunship.

# This is Jedi general Obi-Wan Kenobi.

clone
trooper

Obi-Wan Kenobi
(OH-BEE WON KE-NOH-BEE)

He is using the Force
to lead clone troopers
in battle.

armor

This is Jedi Padawan Ahsoka Tano.

She is using the Force to push commando droids away from her.

Ahsoka Tano
(AH-SOH-KAR TAR-NOH)

# commando droid

# This is Jedi Master Tera Sinube.

lightsaber

Tera Sinube
## (TE-RAR SY-NOO-BEE)

# He is using the Force to fight a criminal.

Not everyone uses
the Force for good,
like the Jedi.

Count
Dooku

Asajj
Ventress

Some use the Force
for evil.
They are called
the Sith.

Darth
Maul

Savage
Opress

Darth Sidious is the strongest Sith.

Darth Sidious
(DARTH SID-EE-US)

He is using the Force
to shoot lightning
at his enemies.

This is evil Sith
Count Dooku.

Count Dooku
(COUNT DOO-KOO)

Savage
Opress

He is using the Force to
teach Savage Opress
how to lift objects.

# Ventress fights for the Sith.

# Ventress
# (VEN-TRESS)

She is using
the Force
to choke
her victims.

# Now you have met the Masters of the Force.

# Who do you think is the most powerful?

# Glossary

## Clone troopers
A group of soldiers who are the same as each other.

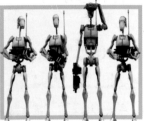

## Commando droid
A robot that is built to fight in wars.

## Gunship
A large aircraft with lots of weapons.

## Lightsaber
A special sword used by the Jedi and the Sith.

## Starfighter
A small spacecraft that is used in battles.